About the Author

Born in the Bronx after the Second World War, Harvey Waldman fled to Northern California as a teenager. Street theatre anti-war activist, dishwasher, farm worker, oil refinery boilermaker, taxi driver, barista, librarian, Santa Claus. Lead actor in 1976 feature film, *Off the Wall.* A father in need of a more sustaining career, he spent over forty years in film and TV production, most recently as Producer of the TV series *Manifest* for Netflix. All while poetry lurked, awaiting its turn—a passionate, unkempt cousin long ignored. He and the film editor Camilla Toniolo have homes in New York and Northern Italy.

Shopping Lists for the Apocalypse

Claire —
my sister on the front lines
thanks for all your support
and GOOD LUCK —
Make more movies!!
love

Harvey Waldman

Shopping Lists for the Apocalypse

Olympia Publishers
London

www.olympiapublishers.com
OLYMPIA PAPERBACK EDITION

Book Cover Art: Concept, Samuel Froeschle; Illustration, Sadra Tehrani

A CIP catalogue record for this title is available from the British Library.

ISBN: 978-1-83543-004-0

First Published in 2025

Olympia Publishers
Tallis House
2 Tallis Street
London
EC4Y 0AB

Printed in Great Britain

Dedication

For Camilla and Luca.
For Jane Gil, Doug McGrath, and Roger Michell,
who left us too soon.
For Jose Mujica, who has led by example.

Acknowledgments

As profusely as dignity allows, I thank Jay Parini for all the encouragement and guidance he provided to make this book happen. Thanks to Jane Bolster and Michael Hoffman for their careful readings of early drafts and for their helpful edits. Thanks beyond measure to Minona Heaviland for organizing the book, as well as her editing, love, support, and inspiration, which often left me wondering who is the child, who is the parent. Special thanks to Imogen Arthur and Amy Cross, at Olympia, for shepherding *Apocalypse* into publication.

Contents

Remember thee?
Ay, thou poor ghost, while memory holds a seat
In this distracted globe. Remember thee?
Yea, from the tables of my memory
I'll wipe away all trivial fond records,
All saws of books, all forms, all pressures past
That youth and observation copied there,
And thy commandment all alone shall live
Within the book and volume of my brain…

– Hamlet, Act I, Scene V

Introduction

By Jay Parini

I've been reading the poems of Harvey Waldman for the past six years or so—we met on a film set in Italy not long after the difficult and fateful election of 2016. I have continued to read the poems, and reread them, with increasing admiration and enjoyment. There is a unique voice in this work, and it calls to me, as it will to many readers.

Waldman has not been a poet on the literary scene throughout his life, but he's been a lifelong reader of poems and his work reflects his attentiveness over many years to the art of poetry. His body of work gathered here reveals his own strenuous effort to find a voice that is distinctly his own but still ordinary, recognizable, as he writes in the rhythms and modalities of everyday speech. That voice, which these poems reflect and embody, is at times richly colloquial, although sophisticated and urban. This is, I would argue, a sharply American voice, and it's distinctly in the mode and manner of twentieth and twenty-first century conversation. One doesn't so much "hear" these poems as "overhear" them.

Shopping Lists for the Apocalypse is a deeply personal collection, with many of the poems falling into a category often called "occasional poems," poems attached to a particular circumstance, such as a birthday or visit from a friend. But that appellation doesn't do justice to the poems themselves, which repeatedly confront the issues of youth and age, looking at mortality with a clear eye, casting (as Yeats once said) a "cold eye on life, on death." One might, in fact, see these poems as dwelling in the line of spiritual poetry, as in the symbolic ending of *The Coleus,* where Waldman writes that he is "happy now to see some pattern" that ultimately involves "room to grow / bigger, fuller, more colorful, and stronger" and drifting toward a mode of gratitude. Or in *The Twelve Stations,* a self-conscious religious poem, where he notes that we have been "sentenced to mortality" but that there is a certain "urgency" to this understanding as we watch "the intercourse of sweat and blood." During this bold transaction, we come to terms with being naked and having to accept our fates.

Waldman is a persistent man, as his poems suggest, and the urge to continue despite the odds against him seems to obsess him, as with *Keep Going,* where he admonishes us all in these terms: "Keep going, each layer uncovered a little / more rewarding than the one before." It's a brave stance in the face of mortality, but the poems here are largely about modes and methods of survival, which is more than simply "getting by." It's about how language often comes into play as we talk to ourselves and find our balance in the world.

There are, of course, some eerie scenarios playing out in these poems, as in the haunting *I dreamt we lived in a Soviet Republic.* The poet imagines "everything shut down," and this includes "the schools, the banks, the buses, the gas stations," and so much else. The poem ends with his hapless travelers in a cemetery searching for the graves of ancestors who seem not to lie there. The reader is left out in the cold, walking a kind of mental plank, waiting "for what was next."

Waldman's settings vary wildly—from the subway in

New York to West London and the Italian countryside: all settings that the poet has made his own, has lived in and learned to appreciate. Subways, in fact, figure importantly in the collection, and they seem as much like symbols as specific spaces in an urban context, drawing us toward key questions: "Where are we going? / Do you really know?" The so-called Final Station lies in the distance, and there is this perpetual journey toward it through the "damp dark nowhere tunnel."

I especially like Waldman's childhood poems, such as *My Family's Candy Store,* which is "fully stocked ready / for business" in a kind of perpetual Bronx that lives forever in a hallucinatory space. The store itself thrives in memory, always available with its delights, with images of the poet's mother and father—Moe and Hilda—burning brightly in the poem, alive.

Life itself figures in many of the poems, a cause for celebration. But our time on this planet is limited, as the poet suggests in *History Lessons from Pandora's Jar,* where he notes that time also unfolds as "a diary of tears." There's fear of mounting crisis, of stakes getting higher and higher. "How do we combat these exponential cataclysms?" the poet wonders. As ever, Waldman sides with the ancients, who believed in "the only God left on earth," which is hope itself.

There are lots of elegies here and elegiac moments. Waldman has lost many friends and family members, lost numbers of places that were dear to him. But poetry, for this poet, is always a return, an attempt to recover what's been lost. He will not succumb to letting indifference take possession of him: "Nature's cruelest act is indifference," he says in *Seeing a photo of Jane watering plants,* which is one of the finest poems in the book.

The poems seek and uncover a kind of jazzy music, one

that fuses with the classical, as in *Listening to Vivaldi.* Music is seen here as a kind of reassembling, a bringing together of distant parts from one's life and psyche, rooting them the flow of a poem, which is always a tune. One hears, everywhere, distant echoes of other poets: Ginsberg, Stevens, Hopkins, and any number of other poets. But these recede as the poems flow, and I think a good reader will take pleasure in the distinct melodies of this work as Waldman weaves in and out of time and memory, as he moves from place to place, from phase of life to new phase, as he looks for, finds, and celebrates the moments in life that become real, memorable—what Wordsworth called "spots of time."

There is also a kind of lively and encouraging note of defiance in these poems. Waldman doesn't want to be left behind, pushed aside, ploughed under. He doesn't want the politics of the Trump era to bury us in their inane loud noises and pernicious attempts to co-opt our consciousness. To this extent, every poem is political in that it asserts a kind of independence, in language, thought, and music, from the prevailing and often imprisoning world of imagery and sound. The apocalypse referred to in the title of the book may indeed be upon us, but Waldman is keeping these shopping lists, showing us ways out, giving us hope, allowing us to live inside the poems for their duration on the page, taking us by the collar, and making us listen. Listen close.

What Is Here?

Poems of captured and framed moments. Paintings: portraits, landscapes, still lifes, pop art, occasional abstracts, but most attempts at naturalism by an untrained hand. Song lyrics without musical notations, but songs meant to be read and heard aloud with instrumentation in accompaniment. Excerpts from books that I will never write, movie scripts, political tracts, memoirs, a history of our times, travel guides, short stories. Recently discovered works of Pierre Menard—was he my doppelganger? Postcards to family and friends, and to you, a complete stranger. Celebrations of birthdays, weddings, anniversaries, or simply daily life. Funeral orations. Meditations on death, advice for living better. Prayers for secular believers. Prompts for action or inaction. Shopping lists for the Apocalypse. Awe at the design and scale of the universe. An amateur's wake-up call to step back from the coming destruction of our small piece of it, the path we seem to be on. Words from a cartoon mouse into a T Rex's ears. Impossibly anachronistic, but there I just imagined, and here, now you've pictured it—these things I wanted to have remembered, to talk about together, or for you to think about when I am gone.

Looking Past Looking Forward

Take the "A" Train

From West 4th, shot out with so much promise
thrust through unseen Manhattan schist
wheels shoot sparks scurry rats
Car's rhythmic throbs of hypnotic whish
mutate as they bend on ancient downtown curves
become screeds of friction track shouts,
overamped dog whistles we pretend not heard
SCReech… SCREECH
back to straightaway train returns
Faster, faster, faster
stop skipped after stop…
Fantastic it's an Express
you think… Brooklyn must arrive in no time!

We approach the river, or maybe as we go under
speed subtly diminishes then slowly stops
Perhaps, the act of going underwater requires caution
Perhaps, it's something worse.

Look around—you're not alone here
not as much alone as you believe
In this crowded home of immigrants
many chose in hopes of getting somewhere better
sit together in the damp, dark, nowhere tunnel
while car lights flash off and on and off
too cold in summer, hot in winter

Eyelids heavy your mind darkens as if
a gauze blanket thrown over head
your vision blurs
the whole sense of… arrival
becomes more abstract.

Where are we going
on this ride that never seems to end
do you really know?
The Final Station always a bit further
trapped in Zeno's paradox
the distances divide in half
then divide in half again
again, and again, the two points never touch
get only incrementally closer
our stops always just out of reach.

'Where's Home?'

Once, there was the Bronx of my parents
from within two hundred miles, they never ventured
having seen their own progenitors
uprooted youths from Hapsburg ghettos
take a lifetime to process their escapes
via steam ships, subways, Fords
to outer borough large apartments retail stores
no need to go any further.
Fall winter spring 50 six-day work weeks
Summer Catskill mountain lake bungalow mah-jong nights
Old Country left behind before the holocaust
Sisters and parents unable to be saved
Looking back not possible; this was now their home.

Twisted genetic strands connect each generation
Boomers replicate once-young Grandparents
seek escape from new 'old country'
East Coast frigid urban decayed sprawls
via Greyhounds, hitchhiked Volkswagens
carry backpacks hear siren calls
Kerouac, Kesey, Grace Slick songs
to Oregon and California, as far away
New York in mind as New York from
Vienna and Galicia sixty years before
The New World was West.

Feel pity for our parents whose bookended generations
rejected centuries of extended families' tradition
Left orphaned, childless, early-onset malignancies
in cookie-cut suburban Jersey shore's desolation row
with neither roots nor next generation for comfort
Heard, "Where have you gone, Joe DiMaggio?"
guess at the song's meaning without understanding
the what how why any of it had happened
not know where they'd gone wrong
only that somehow, they were victims.

For all its primal beauty and Priuses
Alta California life remains uneasy while
piles of mile high kindling grow, built
on fault lines through forgotten native graves
poised one day to ignite and swallow
Inside Telegraph Repertory Pauline's screens revealed
Renoir, Rossellini, Wertmuller, Wenders, Saura
windows to a culture too precious not to savor
Was our real home left behind, almost forgotten?

The world continues to go to hell
Galicia reports of daily shells
History creates each next war inevitable
"From roaming through the earth, and
going back and forth on it"
Satan reports when questioned in the Book of Job
He feels guilty about Frequent Flying
always thoughts of one place while in another
blessed and cursed by these legacies of escape
please don't ask him where his home is
It's here there everywhere and nowhere, all at once.

My Family's Candy Store

Is always fully stocked ready
for business serve late-night customers
returned home stop for a quick
chocolate egg cream pack of Lucky Strikes *Daily Mirror*
birthday card quart of fresh packed Breyer's
in time to catch *I Love Lucy* on new 12-inch
black and white Zeniths.

I pass the newsstand penny candy machines
chained together on the sidewalk
atop the piles of seven daily papers iron-weighted
weather-beaten open cigar boxes receive
trust system payments of dimes and nickels.

Inside's my father smiling to each new patron
or now to me as I walk in
He's got that morning's Wall Street Journal
spread atop the freezer chest behind the marble counter
head buried in codes to decipher
between the lines of numbers
where lies his future fortune
hidden price/earnings ratios missed by all the others.

Here's my mother come out back storage room
always focused on the here-at-hand business
scoffs at his calculations, No,
this is the way we make our living daily

count out fifty pennies, forty nickels, fifty dimes
wrap by hand in rolls for night time bank deposits.

Tall front glass windows display toys we rotate
Easter, Summer, Halloween, and Christmas
being smallest, I'm sent inside them
to handle each season's changes.

I hope Hilda or Moe or some random passers by
stop to take the time to catch each new creation
Roy Rogers riding Trigger throws a slinky around Barbie
Gumby, Pokey, Mr. Potato Head engage in conversation
Dawn Patrol green plastic camouflaged GIs
sneak behind gray horseback knights in multi-painted
armor in formation atop Candyland and Clue sets
Revell model B17s, Battleships, and Messerschmitts
carefully constructed with help from my older brother
wired fly mid-air or ride the seas within
a circled five-car Lionel that runs upon request.
On upper shelf, prized stuffed animals, fancy dress dolls
look down, filled with pride and middle-class condescension,
but rarely sell, too expensive for the neighborhood clientele.

Setting up that world inside those Bronx windows
the closest place to heaven that I've known
Ever ready to return there in my dreams
to watch my parents, re-enact their dance
I would make a thousand chocolate egg creams
and project nothing more than nonchalance.

My Brother Considered Himself a Poet

My brother considered himself a poet but
frightened me his words, references
too internal, oblique, often
mischievous preened in macho poses.

I wanted to be a poet, too
but shrouded in teenage anxieties
never wanted to be like him
I wanted to be understood and
was never sure he did or could.

After Greyhound days, cross-country ride
furthest from home I'd ever been
San Francisco hip summer night sixty-six
eagerly let him turn me on.

Defenseless as a child begun to walk
I ran free on downtown's trafficked streets
flung joyous arms to the Tenderloin
Liberated from the Bronx
Liberated from the immigrant fears of parents
Liberated from need to be anyone other
than who we were, two brothers high
comic book cosmic powered pair
surrounded by suited squares in step

who paid no mind to two long hair
walk among them sight unseen, "We're invisible!" I shout.

"Shush," he commanded,
"you're gonna get us both arrested."

Mystical brother bond in an instant lost
had to straighten up come down fast
He split off to Jefferson Airplane night
left me in closet room Turk Street YMCA.

So, it went—a lifetime of occasional
glimpses of bonding, promises of love
punctuated by paranoia
separate paths to distant ports.

Fuck, if what kept me from writing poetry
dumb for near fifty years, wasn't him alive
busily connect the dots of conspiracies
which lay in traps in his own alleyways.

What had Thorazine and shock treatment done?
Nixon and Reagan, two ex-wives, never enough money
Rogue survivor Nazis, the US Navy, local NPR station
San Francisco Arts Foundation, maybe Ferlinghetti
Were they all in it together?

Joel did better in the woods and seas, moved north
just south of Albion (he'd think of Blake)
Became a fisherman suspended on hallucinogenic
turquoise peaks of green black waters
gray blue cloud-flecked skies around

Pacific in all directions, afloat for weeks
engine off, sea birds, winds, waves only sounds.

On return, one peels from boat for dock
your 'Sea Legs' readjustment time a shock
slow to lose their jelly-wobbled girth
to remember how to navigate on earth.

His battered ship become unseaworthy
unuseful body buried on a Mendocino cliff
When the marine layer's not too heavy
nothing obscures its ocean sunset view.

I like to make visits to his stone
inscribed with his favorite admonition
"No Laughing"
He'd try deliver without a smile
succeeding only half the time.

Left to guess just what he meant
sense him closely watching me
still learning how to walk on land
after so long out at sea.

Looking Past Looking Forward

For Judy

That summer, the A.M. radio played
My sister does the Hanky-Panky
That's what *I* understood when reports came back
from Maryland to my thirteen-year-old brain in White Lake
through the shouts and static:
She's eloped! Run-away! Pregnant!
(did I even know what pregnant meant?)

Old world hand-wringing evidence of this hanky-panky
girl-child becomes girl-woman overnight
Transformed from sister to stranger in-the-world
apartment of her own, a whole other city
a dozen subway stations south
teeming sea of many shades speaking jive and Spanish
so unlike the bland blanketed Bronx cocoon
of our once upon a time.

Soon, her long cross-continent odyssey began
Eugene, Buffalo, San Luis Obispo, Roscoe, Callicoon
resists, then accepts her Catskill roots
entwined bleak winter barren oaks frozen falls
When she can conjure beach trips under
skyscraper coconut palms Capricorn suns
rum and smoke expanded lungs.

When she works, teaches teachers
Challenge special children
watch each go beyond what thought their reach
learn how to listen
where once they'd not been heard
India, South Africa, Ukraine.

Now only memories, escape dreams remain
Sister your body has you betrayed
Hold on to those another day
Take each moment in
Breathe each out a little slow
Let's keep each other company
we're not ready to let you go.

Meeting Charlie

Sometime in early '68
in an old Dodge cargo van
from Berkeley, heading west
University approaches Highway 80
he picked me up hitchhiking
going nowhere in particular.

Herb-fed energy infectious
in the front seat first seemed alone
I'm Charlie just got out from the joint
inhales passes me his smoke
impish grin nod points to the rear
two teen girls in flimsy dress half smile
I toke pass it back turn away
too shy to keep looking anyway
Charlie makes clear he where
attention goes sets the vibes
conversation subject matter
Where you headed, man? Why not hang with us?
the girls are groovy love to party
Come to the City check my music
Weird smiles at them, at me, at them
all happening so fast
We gotta stick together man watch
for the Brothers brought from the jungles
gonna make streets rivers run with blood
I seen it all in jail.

None of that made any sense but still
I wasn't going to bail just yet
how many hippie girls did *I* get to meet?
I knew Berkeley coeds who could talk
Lotte Lenya Marcuse Arendt
they didn't ride van beds getting high
dresses ride up their thighs with nothing on below
nowhere else to be
where does this trip with Charlie go?

Up a flight into rambling once-bourgeois Victorian
eyes adjust to candles incense smoke
filtered light through curtainless, streaked windows
only furniture, pillows, milk crates, sleeping bags
another half dozen bodies, long haired covered faces
none react to our entrance other than make space.

Charlie starts to share his songs
I'm the world's GREATEST rock n'roll-er
songs of jailtime, racial wars
only lyrics I remember
Gonna kill all the piggies drink their blood!
His unmelodic words sung over out of tune guitar
too fucking lame, too filled with hate.

My once-erotic visions of free-flowing hippie sex
could no longer hold me
if to listen to Charlie's music was the price
No one seemed to mind or care as
I walked out and down the stairs
onto Haight Street's string of head shops
soul food record stores Fillmore posters donut holes
tourists' runaways Krishna chanters
in a state of grace

not to know for several years
the fires of hell that I brushed.

Charlie and his followers moved to LA
joined other fallen angels there
chased music contracts movie stars
endured hunger, drugs, rejection, paranoia
Fury's release finally found in ritual blood drawn.

In karmic ring reserved for murderers of innocents
Charlie burns eternal alongside Tim McVeigh
and all the other true believer warriors
Stay thankful his obsession with music
more important than theirs with politics
and he so talentless that I could walk away.

Family Trees

Winds brush past branches as the sound track segues
rustling Maples, Birches, long-gone Chestnuts into
our refugee grandmother's turned pages, corner of an eye
half over us reads her Yiddish *Forward*
We hit White Lake beaches in replayed Normandy invasions
fresh in mythic air, a mere dozen year after
Take that, you dirty Nazis!

College called, the summer of love
Time to change the world, with time left over
for long camping hikes in stoned Sierras:
California Buckeyes, Ponderosa Pines, fragrant Cedars
gnarly Madrones, Manzanitas, prehistoric Redwoods.
The Borscht Belt, a distant toy forest of dimmed memories.

To live outside the law, we were eager
For any day, they might come to get us
Fantasies now our escapes from J. Edgar's boys
hidden in the Oakland Hills among the Eucalyptus.

The old folks frowned. Ignored, they passed away
Nixon came and went. The troops sent home
for a few weeks, we thought maybe the world
would change.
It did, but not in ways expected.

We worked, raised families in exotic lands
neath Lindens, Magnolias, Maritime Pines, even Palms
winds made music in every type of tree
Man, how sophisticated we thought ourselves
how lucky were our children.

Until one unexpected autumn day
The front door opens on their backs
No *adios* just disappearances
attachments to trunks now finished
blown leaves abandon barren branches
while roots cling to their earthly nests
the poor trunk doesn't know what's next
and must wait it out another night.

Gravity

(With Apologies to Alfonso)

Together, huddled in our snug capsule
we check our readings get our bearings
stay on course while hurled through space
Know in the void, we must be careful
small miscalculations lead to disaster.

Come put your ear upon my chest and listen to my heart
She would tell you of the many things you mean to *Her*
Surprised? That my heart prefers to go by she slash her
pronouns of choice for that most easily bruised organ?
Leave *Him* ID for that other one always busy calculating.

Imagination runs free inside our NASA bubble
The Taj Mahal, a Rikers Island cell
a posh suburban home, a parent's apartment
we can't afford to leave or live.

Without you, I am an astronaut adrift in outer space
near panic untethered soon spun out of reach
in eternal airlessness, no one to hear my voice.

I need to stay George Clooney cool
convince you, *Baby, pull me back*
grab my arm be my Sandra Bullock

Inside we'll laugh heat us up some MREs
be content with what we have.

Siri play Cannonball Adderley's Autumn Leaves
Set course for the next black hole
far southwest of Entropy.

Let's find what's on the other side
We've had our fill of this.

On the Occasion of My Daughter's Birthday

Again, the stars align like those
as we reflect upon your arrival then
I played recorder in candle lit birthing room
wanted it to be so natural so
naturally, your mother did all the work
I watched, half in shock
half in pure ecstatic thrill you
miraculous exposed creature
quickly carted off to nursery
eyes closed, mini body bundled blanket
thru glass shell radiant
a celestial Deja Vu pre-eminent.

No random stranger shown
Here was a life already known
That day, today, tomorrow, and ever after
We celebrate this opened portal beyond the stars
unlocked cosmic grandeurs much larger than our
insect consciousness when we remember miracles.

Happy birthday for all of us, but most especially to you
our daughter, sister from the past, our mother of the future.

The Coleus

The coleus on a window sill in my son's room sits
ready to burst its terra cotta vase
Today, I remembered you this age
when we lived together.

The first plant he chose for his own
after a lifetime not showing any interest
growing up in an apartment filled with them
he's taking it with him when he leaves.

Coleus, first ones we two ever had
responded quick to our attentions, rewarded us
with designs perfect for the nineteen seventies
Hallucinogenic blooms of reds, pinks, yellow, greens
patterns more like tie-dyed tees than anything in nature
each coleus unique seems to evoke all others
plant déjà vu "have I seen this one before?"

Strange that I never grew them after we were done
dismissed them as lesser plants too easily grown
preferring difficult ones requiring more complex care
varieties making less attention-seeking color statements.

Some window has been left open
a look into the present which is a look into the past
not unlike being on the street thinking I see Terry

knowing she was killed some thirty years ago
yet here she is laughing with friends
dressed in her favorite torn jeans
railway man's red bandanna round her neck
happily swinging her viola case by her side
oblivious to what happens next.

I want to call out to her, this Terry who is not my Terry.

I content myself transplant his coleus
happy now to see some pattern
knowing what he doesn't
The shock of being forced to move from their old pots
gives them room to grow
bigger, fuller, more colorful, and stronger
and when he survives all that
eventually, be grateful.

Fathers and Sons

Central Park, October 2016

Short cut on the north path late for my appointments
come around an asphalt bend, find there unexpected
manicured soccer fields eerily abandoned
memories awakened.

Warm spring weekend, surround shouts fill the air
Padded dwarf uniformed bodies tumble into one another
Jack-in-the-Box parents poised on picnic blankets
thermoses full of coffees and mimosas
along side lines call boys' names like bids at auction.

My nine-year-old's ambivalent attention in the game
drives his small body intermittent
between mini fluorescent orange traffic cones
Should I push him harder to strike more forceful blows?
In memory, I mimic the latest pediatric advice
offered on the hippest morning shows
Good job, Luc, good job, keep going, kick toward the goal!

Walking to East Side doctors twenty-odd years older
flashbacks compete with present pains
aching feet to shoulders.

Fenced off wrapped in uncaring winds of Fall
suicided leaves spread round now silent fields
I decide to find excuse to give that man a call
cross-reference our two memories, see
what *he* remembers of his boyhood park
Evening's fast approaching, soon it will be dark.

Balls

For My Daughter's Daughter

Gets up, makes the coffee
Rouses children out of bed
Breakfast-ready clothes laid out
Knows no help to come.

He's in the shower
sings shaves gets presentable
She makes everybody's lunch
He fills up the coffee thermos.

Everyone to the cars! It's time
for work for school
The kids learn stay between the lines
always wait their turns
Be polite not get in fights
Remember to clean up after
He's at his office, She's at hers.

Somehow the day's survived, the kids
picked up from after school
Car pools play dates shopping
This evening's prep attacked
She gets done He gets home
just in time for supper.

The kids run to him, it's all very 1950s
He makes himself a drink and says
If you behave after dinner, you'll get Story.

Balls, mutters the Queen under her breath
If I had them, I'd be King.

Knows one day the day must come
She will teach this to her daughter.

The Red Ferrari

For Camilla

In the middle of a country road traversing
the dark enveloped forest we call home
You find yourself tonight the proverbial deer caught
in blinding, bright oncoming headlights
vintage speeding sports car impossibly
arrives round a blind curve at seventy
stand here helpless and transfixed.

When did you stop being Bambi
playful and innocent song birds chipmunks
butterflies rabbits your close companions?
When did everything become so serious?
Fear of hunters replace your innocence?
Joy of life lived in the Now become
fixations on omnipresent dangers?

We know that reckless speeding shiny thing
is ever just around country curves and closer
but on this day, we dare celebrate
the moment of your birth, the start of life
the joyous days and nights of love and laughter
stare down that red Ferrari's fury
defiant raise our glasses
like in fairy tales happy ever after
ti facciamo… tanti auguri.

Greenwich Village Summer Day

As if living in a Film Forum revival
The Day the Earth Caught Fire arrives at last
 forces us to choose how we'll spend our final days
Isolated, trapped inside beneath an AC's roar
or dare venture out to the mad dog midday sun?

I find myself on these downtown streets fascinated
by this plenitude of sixty-somethings out in force
Our Boomer population bubble who
once taught not trust anyone over thirty
now feel caught amidst this corporate campus
filled with youthful resentment of what we've wrought
who don't think we did them any favors

Now's the time to get ready
we fellow traveling hospice workers
Time to change bedpans, administer the drugs
do the shopping, simple cooking
read Kindle books aloud, sing Beatles songs
as lullabies at bedtime for one another
like we did for our own children
To ease the transition
from here to ... anywhere?

A white haired man walks purposefully
down west Third Street towards me

Handsome in seer sucker suit
with artful thin grey stripes
Open-collared pressed white shirt, no T
sweat invisible, stride unbroken as cool as any Brooklyn hipster
I want to stop him demand him answer
where do you get *your* Attitude?
I want me some of that

On a bench in Washington Square
I listen
as a young trio improvises
An audience of pigeons
bop their purple-spotted necks front and back
in time to the alto's riffs on Ellington
Not caring about food just this once
Content to walk around and around in circles
Entranced by all that jazz.

On One Hundred Years of Stan and Fi

A Combined Birthday Toast

Time passes and uncertain
becomes where recall ends and dreams begin
Luckily, we have sense memories
delicious meals, intoxicating drinks, belly laughs
and tears to ground us in the real.

Each autumn, a gazillion leaves crash
from the safety of their branches
to feed the roots they come from
This one slowly rocking itself down to earth
in front of me is special nonetheless
our own red leaf of this moment.

Each evening, a million stars explode above
a billion years ago
There, there's our own incandescent one
that's already disappeared
Time's paradox of floating at the speed of light
That everything that's happened so very long ago
happened just yesterday, just now.

There's no reconciliation possible between loss and love

Only memories to shape them into story
Only art to remind us of the holy.

Oh, Holy Holy Birthdays, one plus one plus one
May they be as numerous for you
as our friends, the falling leaves, the shooting stars above
transported here tonight in this celebration of our love.

How to Write a Resume

If You're Asking Me
Don't Take My Advice
Ray Davies

A resume should read like a Poem
No longer than a page
Never padded with Hyperbole
Work too hard to make impressions
with arcane knowledge, obscure references.

Let yourself be revealed
approachable and user friendly
easily absorbed in single sittings
a little humor never hurts.

A sense of movement always helpful
Inevitable the logic from one season
to next experience leaves a reader assured
I can see that choice.

Times, people, places (yours and where)
Mountains climbed rivers crossed
your place among them clear
A working life palpably felt
bring us to the here and then
leave the reader wanting more.

Trimming the Privet

By mid-July she has gotten out of control
Stems sprout willy-nilly over-sweet flowers
swarm like monstrous tendrils Medusa hair
Hissing snakes writhe coiled
in heat to snare any who would pass
on their way to outdoor shower.

Compelled to sharpen up the loppers
tame this unruly explosion not
unlike late Louie Wain's crazy cats
I climb upon my ladder
reach out as far as shoulders let me
to cut away with pleasure
restore order in our garden.

Can do most trimming by myself
but leave a little section
at high points in middle hedges
for my son to deal with
when he next comes to visit.

Smile in wait for those moments
groans raised brows resistant climbs
he cuts what's left with little gusto.

Yearly I remain persistent

in hopes this dance serves as compost
fertilizer for his future grown
nostalgic for these summer days
when after he works up a sweat
I rate his practiced dives in pool
never less than 9.8.
and many shouts of my approval.

Departures

Talking to a Dying Friend

It was always so
so to receive
prognosis of impending doom
mere confirmation of what we always knew
now come too late to make us worry.

Take a breath
now breathe out
Why bother, you ask?
Why not, is my reply.
If dying makes us question life
we've lived unexamined lives.

Take a breath, now let it out
Try to let those breaths become
your only thoughts.

Think of death as going to a screening
you're just getting there a bit ahead
save our place we're right behind
When we get there, I'll squeeze your hand
You'll whisper in our ears
tell us what we've missed.

Phantoms at Christmas

Covid Time, New York City, 2021

What we give ourselves this year
glimpses over WhatsApp
turns taken visited with invisible bugs
forced to spend this time apart
hold each other only in our hearts.

In our illness being neither here nor there
In our heads somehow in both
for comfort and company see
ghost presences on computer screens
not unlike the way they could
in Victorian seances
cemeteries and attic photos
where transparent hosts appear
faint double exposures linger.

At family gatherings, look twice; there
Franco, Marisa, Joel, Hilda, Moe
we still feel their presence
can speak of them, recall their
joking voices belly laughs so clear
ancient admonishments and threats
all vanished, wasted anxious fears.

Something happens every late December
as the solstice passes
A sign from heaven… daylight returns
each day a little sooner
the sun appears reborn.

So, bonds once made remain with us
not condemned to disappear in darkness
Family stories become family lore
The children always beg for more
we owe to them remember.

Watching Jonathan Winters and Robin Williams on YouTube

"Comedy can be an awful lot of fun, but how would you like to go out, just you, in front of two thousand people and hold them for an hour?"
Winters to Ed Bradley, on a Sixty-Minute Segment

They're in the hills above San Fernando, probably at Winter's
cavorting round his pool, smog too dense to see the valley
having a good time, even the film crew lose their cool
The two comedians free associate
character improvisations, clowns jokes
wild rivers of wit wash the set
with laughter tears of recognition
Stand-up riffs like Zen *koans*
pull down the masks we daily wear.

What price do our comic preachers pay?
We junkies in living room needle parks
think them our private dealers
Entertain Us! Make ME Laugh! Top that with yet Another!
Demand they come armed with
new sets of works each day
ever ready to get ugly
if they show up empty handed.

Sixty Minutes will play forever on the internet
Six million hits and counting
With time, we plainly see their fragility

badly wanted kept a little hidden
They bounce off each other seamlessly
show the oddball in the human
as well as vice versa
Crave laughter keep the curtains open
never want to close the show
Know the hardest act to follow
home alone with home-grown demons
the toughest crowd to please.

Seeing a Photo of Jane Watering Plants

For Jane Gil, 1955–2016

Firm hands conduits to unseen springs
succor the burgeoning garden she's filled
erect, enveloped by her plants, she
looks directly back at us and smiles
indulges us to watch her work for this moment.

We think we could imagine the source
of her strength, knowledge intuition
of what brings life to blossom.

We know we'd be only guessing

Until you've gotten on your knees
shared rock songs with the worms
thrust naked hands through black loamy soil
made rich by methodically nurtured compost
exposed to daily sun and storms
forked over and over to aerate
You can't begin to understand
It is the dirt from which life comes
It is the earth which demands repayment

Night comes upon us now, much too early
left abandoned by her premature departure
so unacceptable, so out of joint
with our view of natural order, we see.

Nature's cruelest act is its indifference.

We rail at the mocking wind, the callous rain,
the suicidal leaves falling compulsively
and we shout back NO, not Jane
you can't have HER, she belongs HERE with us.

Silence

It is the dirt from which life comes
It is the earth which demands repayment.

Searching for Z

Daily, we hack our way through thick brush
in this unmapped jungle
discover nature's latest terrors: noisy swarms of gnats
brown and pinkish pustules ooze
through moonscape skins, itching impervious of relief
We attempt to keep our moving corpses under cover
despite enervating humidity and heat
Fear silent snakes underfoot at each next step
ready to snap at ankles, bring us to ground.
Rat-sized spiders latched onto necks
you're down in sixty seconds!
Paralysis stealthily takes possession, limb to limb to limb…

Exotic diseases invade our companions
one by one, they fall victim
We mourn their loss briefly, then push on
leaving them behind to rot
Who will be the next to go?

Around every bend lurk tribes of painted men
Spears always at their ready,
Suspicious eyes clock our every move
What are you doing here?

What are we doing here? What do we expect to find?
Are the stories of ancient cities of gold, buried treasures

to be uncovered midst these overgrown profusions
merely fables spun to lure us
into quick sands of certain madness?
Or are they truly hidden there,
there beyond the river's next reveal?

It doesn't feel like this will end well
Push on
Though, we know the inevitable awaits
there is no turning back
Push on
Though, we know that heaven's gate
is likely to be locked
We push on.

It's the journey not arrival that matters, so they say
What they mean, my friend, is
be prepared for survival tomorrow
you may have to deal with yet another day.

After a Visit with a Widowed Friend

Clifford Brown, Coleman Hawkins, Dexter Gordon
just the right blend of bebop and ballads
John had fed into the algorithm,
Whiskey Sours and Manhattans mixed
perfectly in tune with all the chatter, music
lubricating the evening's entertainment without effort.

I remember the competition of overlapping voices in their apartment
The two of them, one finishing the sentence of the other
Old stories told so often become performance pieces, duets
crafted down to pauses left for laughs.

Tonight, no music filled the spaces in our quiet conversation
the radio locked onto talk shows
pundits pipe in to fight the empty rooms and solo hallways
that now must be endured
Jeff bravely shows off photo albums recalls
earlier times, exotic places, they'd been together or
even things that John had done alone
art that he'd created, books that he had loved
all now, souvenirs of loss.

How cruel the design and arc of living
First, we struggle to find our voices separate of our parents
feel nervously like freaks

sure they'll be no one to know or understand us
we go out into the world
Touching first one and then another, wonder
could there be someone for me?

Then comes a day, you look right at them sitting in your car
talk of jazz and movies, though
you don't go very far the first time
you count the hours till the next
then the minutes after that
the days turn into decades
it seems the ride will never end; no one prepares us
for what happens.

Be right back, just going to the store.

Left suddenly with silence only haunting echoes remain
to endure this kind of violence you begin your life again.

You Ain't Dead Yet Frankie

You're everywhere you're just not here
From satellite signals, a world apart
word comes of murmurs in your heart
new irregularities new food for fear.
How fragile life how frail how much we take for granted
How would we live if daily lived
our lives like those first COVID nights
paralyzed afraid to leave our shelters.
You would scold such melodrama
but with relief (and WhatsApp)
I can feel your presence now.

Remember the Sinatra concert
Atlantic City supper club near his end?
With cracked voice his songs delivered
from perched signature stool barely wandered.

At a dim lit table not far from ours
A fat drunk Jersey goomba
through nearly every number
half-conscious, cried out for all the world to hear
his encouragement to last with us forever;

You ain't dead yet Frankie!
If looks could kill, Frank's did
    as he went right on singing.

West London Rowers Song

On this random stretch of river
watch the rowers pull their narrow boats
solo or in tandems
not get anywhere in particular
only strive go faster
than they've ever done before.

Stroke, stroke, stroke

The solemn coxswains call urges them row on.

The Thames first goes one way
then daily without fuss or warning
like clockwork changes course
To start out, most prefer to plow
hard against the current
reverse on the flow return favors.

Stroke, stroke, stroke

We are never alone
even in the smallest boat we dream hear
the missing Coxswain's persistent voice
On the Feather!
and begin to ease the pace.

Let's end our days in the boathouse

Brag about our timings, raise our beers
propose a toast.
To all the mariners present
as well as those no longer here
who no longer need to boast
the ones who keep us honest.

Listen closely; you can hear all those drunkards sing

Merrily, merrily, merrily, merrily
life is but a…

Brahms Fourth, an Elegy

For Joel, Again

Majestic calls triumphant brass ominous drums
proceed the return, this time with fanfare
Opening bars of his final symphony's final movement
Mount Olympus Orchestra announces here your presence
arrived in all your vanity and glory
defy nature, modesty, reprobation
Remove the barriers between consciousness and death
your love and recognition needs never met
Come occupy this living room
I know you won't be staying
Raise the volume on the Bose, take it to Eleven.

Spirit, you have no choice but play
pretend conductor forever in my rooms
Earthbound coward, helpless here, I hear your voice
Unable to go forward
Unable to replace this crazy rebel angel's face
who made music for me first
Heaven can't contain these memories you bring
Glory, Glory, Glory, Sing!

Don't Do It

Don't do it.

Don't turn on the television
Don't listen to *NPR*
Don't open your computer or
Take a peek at your smartphone.

Don't start playing solitaire
Or *Angry Birds.*

Don't go through your collection
Of old *New Yorkers*
Photo albums, vinyl records, cassettes, CDs.

Don't think of things you need to do at work
Or look for work
Or check on work, review work already done.

Don't go through your contacts
To find someone to call.

Don't make lists to do tomorrow
Next week, next vacation, or even your next life
Just sit.

Watch what happens.

In the Shooting Gallery

We stand in place, fixed on rolling tracks propelled
Straight-lined next to all the others eyes face front
inexorable our progress sideways in repeated circles
miniature metal clowns identical grins plastered on.

Fate lines up with her teenage children
Chance and Happenstance
Pays fifty cents apiece for several shots
at winning kewpie dolls, takes random aim
Ping!
We hear as first one and then another
comrade has their moment falling down
Ping!
With each turn, there are less of us
Hold your breath; our turns will come.

Remember, at the carnival, it's all a game to fool the Rubes
Each evening the wheel stops, the lights go out
the Carnie resets the clowns, retreats to booze
awaits next day's target practice wickedly hung over.

Tomorrow, round the tracks, we'll spin again
hear more of us get knocked… *Ping*!
Feel sad each time we lose a friend
Wonder, how we came set upon these rings.

Keep Going

Journeys begin with only the destination's shadow
Inspired by memories of some childish thing read
Tentative steps get taken in an arbitrary direction
A spool hits the ground, unthreads, keeps going
You can only know the journey's unpredictable
A trip on unknown roads to distant shores
A brave new world, you're already far from home.

Keep going; one door leads into a room where
stand a brood of Russian babushka dolls
one inside the next
Grandmothers, mothers, sisters, daughters
It's clear they're each and all related
each one a promise of more to come.

Keep going, each layer uncovered a little
more rewarding than the one before
Artichoke petals at first so uninviting
eventually evolve into digestible, less spikey waste
more melts in your mouth meat
the really good stuff you want to savor
until finally reached by feel and perseverance
is revealed the delicious heart
impossibly both soft tissue and hard muscle
whose reward of emptiness and ecstasy
was waiting from the start.

2016 and Beyond

One of These Days, Alice

Mid-winter after dinner, fireplace burning wood
drapes heat like a covered baby blanket
You're hard-pressed to keep eyes open
Someone puts on Marvin Gaye, not heard in decades
Bills pile up… sky high, send that boy… off to die
Make you wanna holler, throw up both your hands.

Flashback to San Francisco: Acme Café circa '74
closing time, weed circulates the walk-in closet
in our early 20s time to shed skins of childhood
Vietnam finally over ready for new paradigms
grow up put away the picket signs become
businessmen, movie stars and healers.

I look at the '70s with nostalgia, John our *working-class hero*
watched Napoleon wave goodbye helicopter to San Clemente
convinced we'd never see again, let out collective exhalations
A good man moved from Peanut Farm to White House
Saturday Night Live, we laughed, *Saturday Night Fever* danced.

We thought our values now woven into nation's fabric
taught our children how progressive change was won
counterculture victories secure, believed
the Gipper just anomaly, Sax playing playboy more the deal
Hollywood lotus eaters in self-absorbed success until
Down the escalator came the Tricky Dickster

from His long exile returned
Not to take him seriously?
America, you've been burned!

Only solution now is to get out new sets of handcuffs
No more making nice, time to bring back Ralph and Norton
make ourselves holler, throw up both our hands, shout
Straight to the moon! and hope it's far enough.

Election Year Picture Postcard

This one's from Santa Monica beach
aquamarine air peppered with native smog
Everything is viewed through a haze of ambiguity
sand sporadically populated with dark-covered mounds
of old clothes and blankets
under which lie sleeping or dead bodies or
just abandoned stuff
no one stops to discover which
It's much too nice a morning.

Cool ocean winds twirl desert air
updrafts lift solo gull effortless in glided flight
suddenly abandon her
furious wings pump
dives breaks water's surface
disappears to search for breakfast.

A single wetsuit surfer catches modest waves
gains more confidence with every pass
joggers range from teens to elderly
carve worn paths on hard sand's surface
beneath the changing edge of tides
Each moves in distinct pace and style
self-possessed assured their virtuous work's rewards.

The distant Ferris Wheel sits silent motionless

too early for the crowds
the Stars and Stripes
already whip full throttle in the wind.

Oh, America, how far you've come
Paradise sits on your Western edge while only
men homeless or obscene amounts of money
seem self-confident they belong
Movie-star wannabes and immigrants
fight to make themselves a niche
The rest appear as awkward tourists

fear they've missed the promised life boats
see too few vest preservers
Maybe there's not enough to share!
Wish they had the beach all to themselves
eye with suspicion anyone comes near.

My Cat and I, Election Night

November 8, 2016

Alfie, yes, like that one they sing of
and I share two homes.

Ravenous at daybreak, he wakes me
with a paw slap on my arm, dangling
off the side of the mattress, still inside my dreams
I reach above to touch the headboards
If they're wooden, we're in the City
If metal by the Bay.

In either place, it's Alfie
announcing in his most demanding way
how he must be fed… Like Now!
No is not an answer; I get up out of bed.

Yawning body length fully stretched
kneads his home's woolen basket walls
unraveled threads compulsively clawed daily
eventually, he'll surprise himself
tear his beloved bed to pieces
left wondering how and why.

Out the corner of his eye watches me watching TV

getting scared to see this *Beetlejuice* reincarnate

As regular as clockwork, his demands for food arrive
daybreak, 1P, day's end, again at nine or ten.

Tonight, we've both stayed up later than usual
obsessed by all the scratching talking heads
in shock at how they all could get it wrong
There'll be no going to sleep tonight without an extra snack
his hunger tracks my restlessness.

Fuck, Alfie's going to wake me too early come tomorrow
I know I'm gonna wish I could be sleeping in
Cats and cacti only creatures unaffected by Dawn's knowledge
He whose name invoked too much actually did win.

Aftermath

It's not easy
Living on your own.

Amazingly, we still listen to the Rolling Stones
more than fifty years of days and nights filled
with Attitude, dude, Attitude
Armed against all Doubts
Posing Pushing back
No squares allowed
Fuck you very much.

Under My Thumb
Look at that Stupid Girl
Tell me whose Fault is that, babe?

What does it mean now that we know
that Mr. T the Terrible loves them too?
His campaign theme song blaring
You Get what you Neeed!
That Male prerogative
is more complicated and universal
than we care to admit?

High and Dry
Up here, with no warning
What a way to go!

John McCain Sits in His Cell

John McCain sits in his cell in the Hanoi Hilton,
concentrating on his breaths
Surrealistic Pillow piped in by his jailors
refuses to self-identify as a lost pawn in a lost cause
uses the lyrics they try to break him with
when he wakes, when he shits, when he receives
his daily bowl of rice
One pill makes you larger, one pill makes you small
His Fellow Flyers look to him for inspiration
The ones that mother give you, don't do anything at all
knows if he keeps it all together, he can still rise
like the legendary Phoenix
His destiny not to rot there unseen, die despised, unknown
To Phoenix he'll return, for surviving he'll be praised
pressed to serve again at home.

His children will stand expectant on the tarmac's edge
poised to embrace him when he lands.

Fifty years have come and gone as in a dream
John McCain for his sacrifice and service
more than once might have become President
instead was libeled by one with racist lies
by another called a coward
Got called coward by Mister Con Man extraordinaire.
Bone-spurred super salesman of himself
fronting his proclaimed *largest crowds ever*

in their hysterical shame, complicitous.

Collectively, the rest of us struck dumb.

Now, among that muted chorus of cowards,
his voice barely louder than a whisper
John McCain sits in his cell in the Senate,
How does he make sense of this final act?
Where will he find
the strength to lift his wings and fly again?

His children stand in wait once more on the tarmac's edge
poised to welcome him when he lands
To come home, rest at last.

I Dreamt We Lived in a Soviet Republic

I dreamt we lived in a Soviet Republic
One day, everything shut down
The schools, the banks, the buses, the gas stations, stores
People wandered in the streets in the thousands
wondering where to go, what to do
The border guards were gone
but the guards from neighboring countries
kept on patrol prevented us from leaving.

Panic seemed close
we had our granddaughter with us
but our grown children were all gone
we didn't know where
electricity, phone, internet, all utility service become spotty.

We all drifted to the cemetery
found many others there too
Looked for the graves of our ancestors for answers
but couldn't find them
waited for what was next.

Viruses Laugh Last

February 2020

Sonoma winter morning fog burns off
weightless California atmosphere
without temperature or substance.

The sun's reign returns
delights the neighborhood cats and birds
remarkable how easy to feel at one
with this climate without resistance.

A single regal hawk tries to perch
claim its throne high upon a gnarly live oak branch
Suddenly, above swarm territorial bands
crows arrive in Hitchcockian numbers
vociferous in voice, protest this intruder
potential killer poised to eat their children
take turns in noisy strafing passes
until the murder's cacophony
drive this nemesis into hasty retreat skyward
their victory-choreographed curtain calls
compete with this morning's radio news
of coming mass contagion.

It's always been like this
Birds crow, cats purr, predators and prey

all voraciously demand be fed each and every day
we masters of the universe
think this here for our amusement.

Nature manages to constantly adapt
change the rules keep evolving
just ask the hawk how it went for *him* today
then ask yourself where we'll fit
on this new food chain on the way
wonder as you ponder it
when viruses begin at last to laugh
what will be their fondest memories of us
receded to the past.

Naked Men

(For the other *Harvey)*

What is it about these men
Drives them uninvited to disrobe?
Shed off outer skins so proud
present themselves exposed
Men obviously quite drunk with power
held over lives of the vulnerable
beautiful and younger.

Their look in mirrors saw
no reflection of rejection, they
closed the doors that held their prey
success make them so blind
believe they'd have their way.

Kept privileges much longer than acceptable
Beg now for sympathy not to be undone
Blame Eve for temptation of the apple
Claims of innocence disingenuously dumb.

Can they really be surprised today?
Long ignored the unleashed fires rage
daily litany of the naming of the names
men of power made finally sit truly naked.
World wide web stigmata *infamato*

These men were doomed from day
of The Nameless one's election
Pussy grabbing narcissist who shocked a nation
With his victory victims hidden swore an oath of vengeance.
(His day too will come.)

Gloves off, we are done with men
who took advantage of a system
that looked the other way
Men who had everything
men who could never get enough.

Saturday Raga

Working week done at last; sleep-in day go slow
think about you over there, here
in our barn, watch morning sun
soundlessly burn off dew fattened grass.

I crave music fill the roaring silence.

For Father's Day, Luca bought a turntable
can now play vinyl unheard in decades
Choose Ali Akbar Khan sitar ensemble
Which, as always, first sounds like tuning up
until melody revealed
Hallucinated Jinns begin to beckon
Where are you, where are you?
and call back *here, here I am*
Round and round
where are you, where are you, are you dreaming?
here I am, here am I, I am here.

How did I get here, what do I remember?
Separated now, one from another
Like stars light years apart in our own spheres of youth
You across an unbridgeable ocean of plague
Me listening now
Listening in the past to this in Berkeley '67.
Would we make a revolution?

Would I get laid?
Would anything ever change?
Would I ever get laid?

Back further to synagogue every Saturday morning
Five years from nine to eleven, chanting parrot Hebrew
Tales we were to live by, picked out by God
among the idol worshiping Philistines
Chosen to smite our enemies, every man, woman, child
who otherwise would smite us, every man, woman, child
While bombs got tested, accumulated aimed at one another
at Public School we trained to Duck and Cover
Don't look out at the windows you'll be blinded melted
turned into Lot's family?
Stay under desks hide your heads.

By '60s Berkeley these no longer our creation myths
Perceived the wider world with different eyes
Rejected everything taught thus as *His Story*
In search of a new *My Story* to identify
Where are you? Where are you?
Whirling faster, faster, psychedelic fueled
break down of ourselves
our ties to family, religion, country
no longer Chosen people
We moved on from our before
music call and response builds
call and responds even more
Building faster, ever faster, ever more.

WE are here, we ARE here, we are HERE (and repeats)
WE are here, we ARE here, we are HERE

We are with each other even when apart
lovers captured by the mysteries of gravity
who never go so far to lose memory
of each other's touch upon each other's hearts.

Yes, maybe that
And yes, but maybe also this
Solitary burning gasses in frozen airless space
propelled random spirals through cosmos grace
merely fixed in proximity to one another's light
each a million light years ago and also here tonight
There you are, there you are, Are you there? (and repeats)
There you are, there you are, are you there?
Now multi melodic music builds to multi climactic refrains.

TAKKA TAKKA BOOM! THEN BOOM!
THEN YET ANOTHER BOOM!

Climax, Echoes, Nostalgia, Silence are what remain.

The Fool

Once upon a time
Intuitive readers could divine
decks composed of cards fantastical
symbol laden archetypes
gave interpretations of a life's breadth
past, present, opportunities ahead
fortunes, dangers, love and death.

Inspired source of illumination
how tragic this mystery art now lost
what remains our are addictions
Poker, Black Jack, Solitaire
obsessive futile money quests
mere mechanical repetitions
What once was sought
as out of reach
as our computers, phones, TV become
the day the Internet crashes
First casualties of the next world war.

Left to stare at black glass silent screens
Future generations will not remember
What it is that they are waiting for
What was it once seemed so essential
from these by then vestigial machines?

I open up those ancient decks
ignorant of what I see
their Kings and Queens don't mean a thing
Hanged Man, Death or Judgement Day
leave me coldly unaffected.

But when The Fool's unveiled
aspect distracted by the distant cock calls of morning
useless possessions drag his walk, dog nips at his heels
oblivious to the yawning abyss where he's about to step,
the whole world feels revealed.

Lady Macbeth Cleans House

Forensically she roams the house
cold sweat junkie combs the couch
in search of one more fix
her labor's sweat outwits each scrub
elimination gives birth to yet another
faint of heart finds the energy to shout
Out, damn spot, out!

Stands back for just a moment, cries
There. And There. There too!
Windows to wash counters dusted
floors in need of sweeping
Gathered garbage to be tossed
Fridge and cupboards inspected
Laundry washed dried sorted
Closets organized, beds made
Errant books put back on shelves
the daunting tasks pile up.

I fear to lose her to this madness
alone to face Birnam Wood's advances
cursed by those damn witches
look for a sign or course of action
Tomorrow I'll get off my ass, if not tomorrow's morrow.

We know Poetry never cleaned the house

though we like to make believe it matters
stare at screens stoked by ambition
fueled by those cruel sirens
who make you pay up front
Who would never make a dime on us
except they know just what we want
how much we love to put off the dishes.

Waiting to Board

Upstairs addressed solicitously on first name basis
served freshly baked in Sky Lounge paradise
Business reps, celebrities, politicians
international one percenters.

Trailed behind strip searched migrants
worldly possessions in frayed baggage
burst through their hand stitched luggage
remains of abandoned homes.

A single mom juggles kids, one in hand, one in stroller
zig zags like OJ through busy terminal untouched
no one pays her any mind
tears suppressed keeps on the move
back east already hears her righteous mom
I told you he was no damn good, no you thought you knew better.

Inevitably, we crash upon delays for our departures
calculate countdowns in crowded corridors
slow-motion nervous waits in limbo
surrounded by resentful strangers.

We line up for our flights
Pray Jesus had it right
It's just here we've got it backwards.

The Wild West

I watch in awe the Moon
that working girl above the old saloon
nightly show herself (or not)
in one of her twenty-eight different costumes
Wonder how she manages make them
seem new on each occasion.

Her moods constant only in their changing phases
capricious degrees of intensity
affect tides naively thought predictable
wash whole belief systems out to sea
waves the size of combines crash
on detritus strewn beaches
our hearts broken
like the pitiful professor in *Der Blaue Engel*
who crows cock a doodle do.

Her pimp the Sun daily flees cross diorama skies
in seasonal patterns that shift horizon to horizon
to shake the cosmic posse off his trail
using varieties of clouds for masked disguises
often disappears mid perambulation
for their love making assignations
We're left to wonder where and when the next thunder
they produce descends upon us.
Their cosmic passions burn down our homes

Forests become farms of ash
Their fluids wash our hills into seas
turn our towns to fields of mud.

I'm convinced they carry on
with one another in different times and places
cavort before sunrises, behind new moons,
during transitions like weird eclipses
conceived, abandoned their bastard children
ancients named the four elements
earth fire water air
who as you'd expect from creatures grown up
without any supervision
do pretty much just as they like
without care of consequences.

Nature's playbook destroys as much as pleases
we crawl inside storm cellars
wait
stuck in a universe of catastrophe and beauty.

After fires and storms, fall 2017

History Lessons from Pandora's Jar

Again, the world hangs poised on a thread
stretched taut by blinkered fools
A quick survey look at horrors past
leaves it hard to decide which time was worst.

14th century Europeans height of the Plague
chances to survive no better than 2 in 5
Century after century of religious wars
exported worldwide by conquistadores
always greater kill machines made previous ones pale
Great War advances murder with unprecedented scale
followed by Depression, starvation, dictatorial rules
poker play with a *second* world war include
'I call your' holocaust's ovens, rape of Nanking
'and raise you' the fires of Dresden and A bomb Nagasaki.

21st century science brings new rapid progress
more killed in great numbers from further distance
Dead lakes, dead forests, plagues of algae, insects
drive desperate people across continents
Whole families, villages, drown before unwelcome shores
Human memories of these few thousand years
reveal our time on planet is a diary of tears
stakes higher with each successive generation
How do we combat these exponential cataclysms?

Only Hope, last creature hidden in Pandora's jar
can imagine any future for children we will bear
Hope builds Resistance, fights despair, creates the possible
though cynics see destruction's delay a last cruel evil.

Hope is the only God left on earth to help us
all others long gave up on men, flew to Mt. Olympus
We the unacknowledged must revise future behavior
harness hope and change to become our own saviors.

Men Often Have Dreams

With Hat's off to Jean Shepard

Though I can't speak for women I assume it's the same
Men often have dreams about winning The Game.
You're just on the side-lines, a spectator too
When the star can't perform, what can they do?
The situation so dire that out goes the cry
for a savior with just the right je ne sais quoi.

Hamlet's dead drunk, fell off the wagon
Pilot's unconscious, plane's altitude fallen
Your Yankees losing the Series, Mickey Mantle is sick
Convention ballot twenty two deadlocked, no candidate picked

Suddenly, everything stops, as if frozen
for over the PA they call out YOUR name
Crowd all a flutter, buzz Who is *that* guy?
You walk down the aisle with calm answer plain:

I've memorized 'To Be or not…', know all the soliloquies
Seen 'Flight' more than once, landing is no mystery
I'll wait for my pitch to come over the plate
and be honored to serve this nation so great.

It's how we all get through each trying day

as we patiently wait the big call to come
The one that invites us to join in the play
take command of the game ball now in our palm
receive the crowd's cheers, return the high fives
because we're all secret heroes who live secret lives.

La Mia Vita Italiana

Venice, New Year's Eve

Through thousand-year-old streets, thronging tides
of mostly young black-clad enthusiasts flow out against us
Stubbornly, we navigate our counter clockwise direction
tonight, only two not compelled to make the pilgrimage
witness the multi-colored, noisy necklaces unveiled
above, annual proof of humanity's superiority to the gods.
Across the frigid sky, luminescent glows
the dim, distant planets, stars, and constellations
eclipsed by Promethean displays of *fuochi d'artificio.*

Scores of shuttered stores brightly illuminate their wares
the worst and best the West has here to offer:
Feathered rhinestone-covered masks for Carnivale,
made in China lace, the latest Prada, Camper, Timberland
St. Marco Square and Gondola refrigerator magnets,
colored vases by Venini, tall Harry's Bar Bellini glasses
Kitschy tees read: *I don't need Facebook I have real friends*
the ubiquitous phone stores: Vodafone Telecom Wind
In the oncoming human wave, none over 10 without a cell
Camilla threads arms squeezes hands so as not to fall.

Inside the churches, images of holy reverence
mix in with tchotchkes
One wonders if it wasn't always thus or just
one of the modern wonderments of plastic

Would it be the same if suddenly one found
one's body amidst the Hajj?
Walking clockwise around the Kaaba
white-clothed pilgrims rush, push past us without pause
ignore us brazenly go in the wrong direction
intent in their own journey's reward
certain of the communal ecstasy that awaits them.

Do they sell tchotchkes in Mecca too?

We make turns off the crowded streets
find ourselves alone
An ancient deserted silent square
all windows darkened shuttered fast
Perfetto! I hear a Production Designer sigh.

Midnight's come at last!
Celebration sounds emerge from the distance
firecrackers, cherry bombs, cheers, cries,
clanging pots and whistles.
We grab each other's hand know our
escape safely made from our imaginary pursuers
Barely see each other's face join to kiss
embrace silently make our wish
Dare the gods let us have this moment forever.

The Morning Rush

Slowly *con calme* shower dress
as if *un po di stile* called for
downstairs at our corner café *Ficopalo*
order from Giuseppe *Un cappuccio*
e un cornetto con pistacchio
It only costs three euros
reason enough to love *Milano.*

At outside table watch
the world pass in all directions
here mostly populated by purposeful
women intensely concentrated
on foot, on bikes, on *motos*
going where they need to be
usually just on their own
occasionally with a child in tow
sometimes in groups of two or three.

At the bus stop right across the street
a black and white poster *La Vittoria e il Pugile*
a statue of a winged woman on a pedestal
below her sits a half-naked, muscular man
head in one hand held up on bended knee
who seems a little out of sorts
A little on the nose, I swear
the poster's really there

but what could it be selling?

I invent backstories, destinations, desires
first for one, and then another as she passes
The Girl from Ipanema plays
in the soundtrack in my head.

Guilty pleasure restlessness curiosity all scramble
Eyes follow east and west
east again
So much Beauty, so much Will
Queste belle donne Italiane,
Ahhh!

It Begins Here

Around eleven, when weather permits
weekday mornings, a wonderful *spettacolo*
Two dozen or so pre-schoolers
joyously explode from next door's *asilo*
Free Time! to play or roam
play structures, trees, a little winter garden enclosed
safe space falls meet earthen floors
separate in groups of three or two or four
A set of twins identical in fashion conscious dress
matching red scarves, hats, blue coats, yellow boots
seem to like to stick together, though
you suspect this they'll eventually outgrow.

One child by himself, head tilted, almost frozen
Tangled, nappy hair piled high as a potted shrub
hand held near face to chew what looks like stick
silently observes the others without movement
Two teachers observe him huddle
One goes with generous hug embraces
hard to say if he responds
Another boy leads a mini group of followers
with much too much machismo
Teacher two admonishes this poseur's posture
pack quickly abandons *il piccolo signor maestro*
    twins run over to the solo child, who just ignores them.

After what seems too little time
playtime's over, children rounded
all except our only child
who patiently waits to be gathered
his teacher gently leads him
through the doors
to join with all the others
left behind the monkey bars
abandoned leaves in unperturbed whims.

Were the children just imagined?
Weather hopeful will return them all tomorrow
to watch more of the future
unfold here below our window.

4:54A Milano

Walking sleepless hallways induces a headline flash:
Our poetry is nothing more than shopping lists
Inventories of fears and fantasies
Unanswerable questions
No use to anyone; certainly not Camilla left in bed.

A single siren's refrain breaks the night's silence
Whose pain has caused this flight?
Broken some social contract summoned
authorities to set things right?
A solo Carabinieri racing home
before the morning traffic jams
warm brioche on car seat to surprise his wife
Perhaps his mistress called to threaten
his outing without a late-night visit
Hauling ass on Corso Italia
squad car running out of breath
Merda merda merda corri corri corri.

How much longer do we have
How much more can we endure
How can we sleep knowing
How intensely life feels insecure

Death angels skydive nightly over Kiev
Crowded arks capsize short of Lampedusa

Children in the Holy Land eat bread made out of stone
While in apartments on Via Montenapoleone
Rue de Rivoli, Hampstead, CP West
uncomfortable privilege tries get its beauty rest.

Let's make shopping lists for the apocalypse
the practical will want
lists that grow large fast
olive oil, coffee, onions, matches,
change of clothes, batteries, guns
in the USA, lots of guns.

My list is of another kind
If it survives the cataclysm to come
Starts with compassion in our hearts
for all living creatures that still remain
No separate nations, armies, money
No calls for any vengeance
saves competition for sports events
to create a world that honors culture
music, poetry, comic books
these most important for survival
these reasons enough for renewal.

Sardegna Summer

Nothing could be as still as this heat
brushed breeze barely washed ashore
staccato songbird's solo sounds
varieties too impossible to count or to ignore.

Competing? Seducing? Warning one another?

Human voices drift up from the neighbor's house
hidden in the pine forest between us and the sea
Vieni qui amore, vieni qui.

Off shore a single sailboat its siren song mute
White wind-shaped concave canvass
too far away to hear, her
bow ploughs receptive waters
stretched to horizon as unbearably blue
as the deepest lapis.

The sky and sea some five hundred-count cotton fabric
draped moisture over every pore
of our skins, our eyes, our lips
smother all senses until no separation desired
Separation still remains.

Never mind the warmth, the breeze, the perfect views
the funny drinks, the absence of foreign news

When paradise on earth, we come across
Our minds work like the Sorcerer's Apprentice
Juggled doubts, memories quickly multiply
overwhelm un-conductible chorus of ambivalence
music gone maddeningly awry.

Competing? Seducing? Warning one another?

Basta, there's no more need for this
Shut up and listen to the silence fool
Leave the brain noise all alone
The breezes softly whisper past
If you listen hard enough
you can hear her call come through.

Come here, my love, come over here
I've been waiting here for you.

Back Roads to Far Places

With a Nod to Ferlinghetti

On the village street today, I found myself amid
a pastel pack of shorts and socks with sandals
shuffling, darting eyes, wondering where to look
A garrulous guide, raised elongated selfie stick
and book, leads them up the *Duomo* stairs,
Can anybody hear me there?

At such moments, the solo traveler generally
checks out his cultivated air of superiority
cached like a prophylactic in his backpack
for occasions such as these or sudden rain storms
packed carefully between his poncho, water bottle, snacks.

Hard to watch your fellow travelers
carry home cultures with them everywhere they go,
Oh shoot, we're missing the new Game of Thrones
take a plethora of photos, but never get to know.

Walk up and down the earth with eyes wide open
trust your instincts to lead you to the new
take chances down blind alleys
never be afraid you might get lost.
What you miss is easily made up for
what you find all on your own belongs to you.

Heaven

Is a place you've imagined
as Having it All: a pain-free body
In climate-perfect world, *sirocco* breezes
blow gently in your face atop hillsides
high above deep blue glass surface waters
matching lighter shades of skies, cotton ball clouds clustered
on horizons softened wondrous open vistas.

Something like where we are, here in Ravello.

Ravello, of course, with no traffic or other tourists.

Gliding over carved hill curved coastal roads
in an open Alfa, at your side, Princess Grace or Di's
long hair whistling out the windows
laughs at all your witty stories
Fed seedless grapes hands-free by
suckled poolside virginal girls or boys
(depending on your tastes)
Monteverdi madrigals piped in
your every whim anticipated catered.

Perhaps, better to reframe this imagined
stay in Heaven probably wouldn't be like this
walk in the park Sunday drive or picnic
Nothing physical remains with us right? No skin

no body senses where nothing ever changes
no seasons hair styles no outside, only in
No softness, no southern winds
no convertibles in Heaven, dammit!

What's left… Spirit? Particles or waves?

It might be Heaven but doesn't sound like Paradise
Hard not to think in such a place
you wouldn't get a little restless
I'll take my walks instead, from Ravello to the sea
Ride the crowded bus back home, enjoy this scenery
try to forget about what's After
like they say… it can wait.

In the Atrani Church

After the steep climb down from Ravello
you find the church at the entrance to Atrani
a spacious cool enclosure protected from the heat
an illusion of floating in an open space of white.

Sit on a wooden pew guarded by coral columns
framed in green, black and white speckled borders
falter on the marble floors discover patterned
Stars of David drawn down the center aisle
amidst the rows to back wall of the altar
where Mary holds center stage as she so often does
flanked by a pair of martyred saints unknown to me
but surely not parishioners who worshiped here for centuries.

There's intimation of a Heaven hiding high above
Sun-lit stained glass reveal bas relief leaves and flowers
The center panel a single painted mural
haloed Mary stands adored by Angels
a single dove mid-air, backlit by a golden star
flies over a large throne of clouds where sits above
The Father and His Son.

Don't most men wish to reunite
with their long-lost fathers?
After lifetimes passed without them
look up, ask, *Father, can you help me?*

How do I know the straight path from the others?
A prayer that must often have been made here.

But, uh-oh, now here comes a Sister
emerge from the shadows
like in the final scene of *Vertigo*
to clear the church.
Closing time for *pranzo*, Lunch!
Not time for prayer but time for moving on.

It seems we're not meant to find answers here
Today, but here find inspiration
For the search for what we think we lack
requires more than one morning's meditation.

Our Anniversary in Ravello

Grape leaves sparkle in morning's light
Water drops from yesterday's storm shimmer
Diamonds placed on green velvet pads displayed
in the jewelry market, shelved beneath coral-roofed
hills terraced to distant, liquid lapis-covered skies.

Licorice perfume laces the air
My nostalgic Bronx nose wonders if there isn't
a Good & Plenty factory nearby
A neighbor's rooster unleashes cartoon calls
reminding us whose home this is
I bow, thank his salute for our most delightful stay.

Below the road you take to work each day
I see into the garden you thought abandoned
for the season
fruit overripe fallen to the ground
A young African man works his way
through the windswept field
picks every remaining tomato
into a basket improvised with his shirt.

I hope you're right
that no farmer still works that field
that no one besides me notices
that the rooster can stay quiet.

Certainly, in this fertile place
There's enough left for him to glean
He's most likely feeding friends
or perhaps his traveling family
He sees me see his little haul
exchange our complicit smiles.

Today, a sweet day to remember
I'll tell you all about it when
you get home to the dinner
I'll make for us tonight.

Listening to Vivaldi

We see skipped stones surf river's surface
Defy gravity etch paths of concentric circles
in all directions, spread
as if to mark possession.

Half-hidden patient amphibians wait for us to tire.

Our bodies tumble down idyllic hills
crush overgrown grasses into oriental carpets
Grasp giant sunflowers' outstretched stems
in their turn, reaching for the nearest star.

Music re-assembles our imaginations
Surrounded by water, wind, green and sun
Ears first, fast upon them our mind's eyes
create patterns we can see as well as hear
Things we didn't know we knew
the architecture and geometry of nature infinite
reproduces surprise wondrous recognition
of harmonic wordless transportations.

Electrons and their nuclei, flowers, birds, and bees
salmons swim upstream spawn
after years exiled in distant seas
Penguins constant sit on their snow-lashed eggs
Somalian families in overcrowded boats

Earth precarious in its solar system
Chaos and structure live one inside the other
create their rhythms from their needs.

The palace walls are richly decorated
We dress in our finest while candle lit
perfume masks the un-sanitized anarchy outside
In here reside the fortunate, the world aligned just so
A mathematical pastoral dance, *tempo moderato.*

The Twelve Stations

(Above our house in the *Piemonte* hills, looms the *Santuario di Montespineto*, a church and retreat built centuries ago. Leading to it, alongside a steep, winding path in the woods stand a series of small chapels, each painted with images from the stations of the Cross and after.)

That you had always been condemned
sentenced to mortality was understood
Now begins an urgency to this knowledge
each next step you take
brings you closer to that fulfillment.

Each with our own burdens, crosses we carry
distort our bodies, twist our gaits with
failing limbs or organs, cancers, so many
types of cancers, incontinent aging parent,
children stuck halfway out the door.

Everyone falters with these, stumbles to the earth
as they maneuver the awkward hefts of
that which throws them off their balance
begin to accept that even the smallest steps
of this last short journey will be painful.

Imagine your own mother
what she must have felt when you

young, wild, obnoxious rejected her completely
Surely now you see upon her face
the pained expression of her helpless love.

Among the rubbernecking crowd in witness
of the walking accident your life's become
you hope someone else to come with
sufficient strength lift some share of weight
from off your tired shoulders.

Somehow you continue
the intercourse of sweat and blood
leaks from your body
A stranger on bended knee
wipes with her poor cloth in hand
these your last progeny for them not to be
abandoned on cold stone streets in Jerusalem.

To receive such unsought kindness
reason enough again to falter
find lips kissing dirt you rise
crowned brow cut with thorns confess
the liberation you seek demands full
payment in blood, nothing less.

In this moment of clarity smile stoically
to give some hope to others
Perhaps a gesture to the loving women
in your life beside you to your end
brings *them* some small comfort.

This last move brings you down *again!*

As in all comedies, falls work best in threes
There is certainly no turning back
no escapes or plot reversals.

Time to shed the last illusions
all remaining garments shorn
naked accept inevitable your re-enacted end
clever denials can't prevent your martyrdom.

The last painful accusations
each now nailed into place
This the way your world ends alone in agony
witnesses struck dumb
while paid soldiers do each next Emperor's bid
millennium upon millennium.

Along with the common thieves close by
embrace death expect no miracle relief
Our cries go unanswered by our dead fathers
close your eyes accept your fate.

Simple souls and children see beauty best
babes at mothers' breasts, daffodils return each spring
fireflies light summer fields, dolphins sing beneath the seas
We pray angels watch from stars above
Now I lay me down to sleep…

Winter Solstice

In this quiet moment, through my frosted window
see fifty miles to horizon's snow-capped Alps
Heat of the wood-burning stove
warms me through this second skin of cold
Arctic air which surrounds
this land, this house, this room, my body.

The ice storm just passed snapped dozens
of mature oaks in just one night
as easily as kindling
Too hot and dry the summer, autumn left
too many off-season dead-leafed trees
capture ice-laden branches
too heavy for the trunks.

Kerack!
Just like a comic book balloon
echo trees split in two or several pieces
We've begun the process to remove them.

Struck standing in this cold, silent moment
knowing one day that I won't be
Cold and silence reminders of the inevitable
Will it come upon us quickly?
With no time to pack or petition an extension?
Kerack!

Or drag on painfully until one begs family for relief
the approaching lack of senses seem a solace.

The trees have broken, but the mountains are unmoved
new trees will get planted, or perhaps they won't.

It will be up to those now children still standing on this earth
on that day, we have been waiting for
from the moment of our birth.

From Here

As hilltop winds whisper warm kisses on your face
gentle sea waves rock you side to side in rhythm
I wish these words would transport you
to this place of constant, unfurled vistas
begging comparisons to famed Olympus.

From here, between the clouds, sun's reflections on the sea
create sparkling floes migrate across the surface
Entwined mirages, more like ice than water
Pleasure boats, coiled random pearls congregate together
seek comfort in the harbor near to one another
a colony of ants in an inviting Italian kitchen.

From here, one understands why the ancients
worked so hard and built so high
Frightened animals obsessed with stalking danger
always lurking, who sensed their roles as prey
From here, they could see in all directions
know from where the next invasion might be on its way.

Today's predators snuck in under guise of easy money
seeking pizza, tchotchkes, selfies and Campari
They've proven more difficult to fight
The locals who've been doing this for centuries
pass on to the children this important lesson:
Keep the roads too narrow for Americans and Germans

Leave no spaces free for them to park their cars
From here, eventually we'll bid them arrivederci
go back to counting up the stars.

Postscripts

Dear Alfie

From far off Santa Rosa words come cry
of your decline, pained mobility failed kidneys
inability to eat your canned food loved
through too many uncounted years.
As you approach twenty in our lives
how do we calculate yours?
Would we know how much longer you'd survive
if we actually understood cat math?

You became the shut and opened door
to mysteries otherwise likely gone unexplored
showed us how creatures other than our kind
can choose live independently as possible in
never ending moment to moment calculations
to get what they desire, even when what they desire
includes affection on a daily basis.

In that exchange you provided constant pleasure
excitement at every door of everywhere we lived together
stalk the mice in our apartment, bring their corpses as presents
even after long futile chases of suburban rabbits
exhausted arrive curl up at our sides expectant
vibrations purr out mutual rewards our fingers
knead well below your fur in deep massages

Our trans-oceanic follies not a life for you

decide old American mantra best
"Go west young cat!"
Pack you off to travel that way cats now do
pills put you under our Delta Business seat
you slept all the way and then some so
I worried all day and night that you OD'd
You woke up to live the California dream
cat door onto large fenced richly vegetated garden
no more frost or snow for your complaints.

Minona tells me that now she cooks you
"human" food fresh chicken, fish, veggies
to share along with her family
this the only food you can now digest
canned food inedible, reject, regurgitate
who could blame you after so many years?

Every desire we chase involves another sacrificed
along with this comes acceptance of the sadness
we might not cross paths again
Happy hunting, Alf… next life when you can
I don't need to tell you twice
Catch us a nice fat rabbit… we'll put up the rice!

Not Quite in the Rocking Chair

Our internal mirrors manage to reflect
self-portraits invisible to the world
negatives from years ago
taken at some crucial point
Full head of hair, certainly no signs of gray
waist sizes, several pairs of numbers lower
memory much sharper.

Down small-town streets mid-America or Italy
de populated of all but the most elderly,
old men and women radiate stink eyes at me
I think they think as I pass by
Long-haired, dirty hippie, what's he doing here?

Have I gone mad? Lost my sense of sight?
My clothes all city new and clean
What little hairs now left on me
all practically quite white.

You shouldn't be surprised to hear
my self-image frozen at twenty-nine
Weren't we the ones to once shout loud
and clear: trust no one any older.
So much of what we see
are our fears projected on the world.

Underground, 2023

We descend the stairs cards turnstile swipe
those who can't afford to simply jump
Subway vibes '50s cool in black and white
wheels rub tracks thread bass line throbs
Captive audiences sway silent dance communal
feign disinterest as best attitude for survival.

Each takes our preferred place by rote
travel up or downtown to carry out
the daily tasks that make up our lives
scan cars like private eyes or spies
calculate the odds on each of the possible
two million interactions for potential trouble.

Here ride together the successful and the lost
those still on the make and those now tossed aside
enveloped in the public isolation that defines the City.

Yes, it's true about New York
If you can make it here… you can make it anywhere
But what if… you can't make it here?

First warning sense is often that of smell
harsh witches brew of mold and feces unmistakable
Soon, grunts obscenities break through
what was thought inviolable fourth wall

now completely broken our pulses quicken
Fuck, what's about to happen?

The black and white world racks into color
an apparition of wounded survivors
descendants of the domestic strangulation
that was slavery, followed by Jim Crow
There's nowhere safe where they can go
This false shadow of a railroad underground
leads to no escape, no somewhere better
With no reparations come their way
volcanic primal anger festers.

Help Me! Stay back! Help Me! You all are Killing Me!
I don't care! Kill Me! Kill Me! I'll kill you all! Kill Me! Or I'll Kill You!

Black man-child orphan once worshiper of
Black man-child superstar of song and dance
Jordan would imitate for pocket change applause
those hopeful days replaced with homeless paranoia.

Of all the others who could have sat in his space this day
Fate placed White man-child Daniel
Marine vet ready to serve again if duty called
Where had been his thanks for this where
was even a fucking job like tending bar
Where was he even headed? What was he living for?

I don't care what happens to me. You all are Killing Me!
No, no, no, you won't. I'll kill you all. Help Me! Stay back! Help Me! You all are Killing Me!

I don't care! Kill Me! Kill Me? I'll Kill you. Kill Me?

Screaming voice in their faces louder than
screeching tracks beneath their feet.

MAKE IT STOP MAKE IT END
silently they prayed inside looked away

Daniel reacted as if obeying orders yet
neither Daniel nor those around him knew
how to stop himself stop himself
squeeze shut Jordan's breath
last excrement oozed out of him
over subway floor, spread toward their feet
All backed away to witness death.

Embolden now our better angels
tag with us these tiled walls
E Pluribus Unum
exactly as our money pledges
to build a City of Second Chances
create jobs for our returning soldiers
safe passage for our crazy dancers.

Walk past the yellow safety ledges
board the "A" train home again
look each other in the eye
know we are each other's friend.

September

Unprepared overnight the atmosphere breaks
what seemed our permanent condition appear
like so much that happens in our lives
met with a mix of fear and relief
disappointment at
all the plans left undone or not attempted
We bitched and moaned throughout summer's heat
the crowds, the impossibility of easy travel
now like some bratty know it all crow
we knew all along was too good to last
beer pong cheers in the pool replaced
by needs to dress in layers, rake the leaves
children all return to school
left to wonder if they're happy to escape us

Soon enough this season too be missed
we'll be nostalgic for this passing
perfect blend of warmth and cool
redolent with nostalgia, hopeful expectations
There's time enough to mourn winter's come
Noon church bells ring in cascades of celebration
time to be simple

www.ingramcontent.com/pod-product-compliance
Lightning Source LLC
LaVergne TN
LVHW041213090325
805508LV00002B/279
* 9 7 8 1 8 3 5 4 3 0 0 4 0 *